snooker

THE DICTIONARY

British Library Cataloguing in Publication Data

Haselden, John
The snooker dictionary.
1. Snooker—Dictionaries
I. Title
794.7′35′0321 GV900.S6

ISBN 0–7153–9066–X

Typeset by Vine & Gorfin Ltd, Exmouth Devon
Printed in Great Britain
by Redwood Burn Ltd, Trowbridge, Wilts
for David & Charles Publishers plc
Brunel House Newton Abbot Devon

Published in the United States of America
by David & Charles Inc
North Pomfret Vermont 05053 USA

snooker

THE DICTIONARY

BY JOHN HASELDEN
ILLUSTRATED BY JOHN HEADFORD

Everything you always wanted to know about snooker
— and more!

DAVID & CHARLES
Newton Abbot London North Pomfret

RULES

Equipment: One TABLE, one SPONSOR, two ASHTRAYS, six TV cameras, several logos, a large cheque-book and a lot of BALLS.

Players: Sometimes, but mostly Embassy, Benson & Hedges or Rothmans.

Competitors: Usually two, each armed with a long CUE whose tip needs to be slowly and carefully chalked before each shot, just in front of the ADVERTISING hoarding with the biggest logo.

Object of the game: (i) To focus the camera for as long as possible on the words Jameson's, Coral, or Lada.

(ii) To see how long WHISPERING TED LOWE can go in any one frame before he takes a sharp intake of breath and sighs: "Oo, good luck mate."

(iii) To buy a Porsche, some neat THREADS, a BUNGALOW in the country, and get as far away from ROMFORD as possible.

Winning the game: The player who, in the opinion of the sponsors, has spent most time using his ashtray, shall be awarded the championship. First prize is the exclusive opportunity to mention the venue of one's next exhibition match in a 30-second interview with David VINE.

Accountant A man in a grey suit who knows somebody at the Inland Revenue who likes a drink.

Actually A word used to separate the beginning of a David VINE sentence from its end.

Accountant

Advertising Extremely large and colourful hoardings of cigarette logos, kindly loaned by the manufacturers to the BBC for the duration of the tournament in order to save the corporation from wasting public funds on expensive scenery.

Advertising

Aitch — Diminutive soubriquet for Howard Kruger, manager of the FRAMEWORK team, and one of the few serious rivals to MR BIG, Barry HEARN.

Ambidextrous — The type of multi-talented player who is able to play, smoke and accept BAULK CUSHIONS with either hand.

Angles — A MANAGER's clever methods of fine-tuning a CONTRACT, to make sure that over and beyond mere appearance money, his player benefits from the inclusion of such essentials as five star hotel accommodation, a limo and a good-looking BALL MARKER.

Ashtray — The star attraction at several major tournaments – or indeed at any tournament in which Alex Higgins has been invited to smoke.

Autobiography — The story of an 18 year old's life, ghost-written by a News of the World journalist after the lad wins the BIG ONE. Available from any book shop specialising in remainders or from the Bargain Book section of any branch of W. H. Smith, the slim volume is a good buy if your snooker table has one leg that needs just a little bit of propping up.

Autograph — A player's signature, appearing on CUES, BALLS TABLES and the packaging of international FRAGRANCES, in exchange for a small consideration. See also ENDORSEMENT and GENESIS.

B

Backhand	With which a player picks up a BAULK CUSHION.
Ball	Some people say snooker is a load of balls. They're right. There are fifteen reds, a black, a pink, a blue, a yellow, a brown, a green and a white.
Ball Crusher	(i) An affectionate nickname for Len Ganley, the giant referee of Carling Black Label COMMERCIAL fame. (ii) A less than affectionate term for a painfully overweight BALL MARKER.
Ball Marker	A GROUPIE with sharp teeth.
Baulk	A player's reaction to the discovery that his exhibition match at the Batley Working Men's Club is not going to result in quite the size of cheque he was at first led to expect.

Baulk Cushion	A brown envelope sufficiently large to overcome this reaction.
Bender	(i) A trick shot that swerves. (ii) A waistcoat lifter. (iii) What a good Irish boy goes on after losing the BIG ONE.
Big One	(i) The EMBASSY World Championship. (ii) The first of many references in this book to Tony Knowles.
Billiards	A version of snooker that takes less balls.
Black Ball	Too much BALL MARKER.
Blue	(i) An Aussie snooker player, often well GUTTED. (ii) Definitely not WILLIE Thorne's favourite colour, after a disastrous miss of an easy pot in the 1985 World Championship.
Blue Ball	A painful physical condition resulting from a player being left out in the cold after a GROUPIE has refused to come up and see his CUE EXTENSION.
Bollards	Term of greeting for a traffic warden booking the CADILLAC outside the CRUCIBLE.
Bolton Heart-Throb	(i) A cocktail popular with the 18–30 age group. It's stylish to look at, with a lot of body, but there's nothing much on top. (ii) Tony Knowles's nickname.
Bottle	(i) The nerve to go out and earn £60,000 for ten hours' play. (ii) The nerve to avoid giving the cheque to your MANAGER as soon as you've got it.

Baulk Cushion

Bottom	(i) Type of twist applied to a ball to keep it rolling. A painful technique in the wrong hands. (ii) All the camera sees of Bill WERBENIUK when he's on the table. (iii) All the camera sees of Bill Werbeniuk's glass when he's off the table.
Break	(i) A few pots in succession. (ii) A few days in Tenerife. (iii) A few days in hospital.
Break, Maximum	(i) Big damage at the table. (ii) Big damage at the hotel, to the sponsor's plant pots, or to the BRIDGE of an official's nose.
Break, Tax	Successful negotiation by the ACCOUNTANT, whereby a player's income is taxed at a lower rate in exchange for two exhibition matches at the Inland Revenue Snooker Club.
Bridge	(i) What a player rests his cue on when he's trying to sink the pink. (ii) The part of an official's nose that most comes into contact with an Irish player's forehead.
Broker	(i) An investment analyst. (ii) How a player feels after settling out of court for a MAXIMUM BREAK.
Brown, Sink The	It's what your right arm's for.
Brylcreem	(i) How players and referee John Street used to keep their hair in place until the advent of gel. (ii) Jimmy White's opinion of Nivea.

Blue Ball

C

Cadillac	A wide American car much favoured by GINGER GIANTS. See also STEVEMOBILE.
Cannon	A person who plays religiously.
Catastrophe	The only word big enough to describe what happens when Steve Davis loses the World Championship or Barry Hearn loses his wallet.
Chalk	What the barman uses on the SLATE.
Champion, The People's	Characteristically modest title assumed by Alex Higgins upon winning the 1972 World Championship.
Charisma	That undefinable personal quality – you've either got it or you haven't – that lifts the GINGER GIANT right up there alongside Nigel Mansell as Britain's most magnetic sporting personality.
Chump, The People's	Popular corruption of Alex Higgins's title.
Circuit	(i) The relentless tour of provincial snooker clubs, social clubs and working men's clubs, building up a player's reputation. (ii) The relentless tour of provincial night clubs and illegal drinking clubs, demolishing a player's reputation. (iii) The type of judge this player finds himself up in front of.

Cannon

Class	(i) What you've got when you can play the best of 35 frames in half a dinner suit without spilling a drop of the SPONSOR'S PRODUCT on it. (ii) What Jimmy White and Tony Meo skipped so that they could travel the country with DODGY BOB, snooker impressario and part-time taxi driver.
Classic	(i) An absolutely unique tournament, so distinctive in its image, style of trophy or size of prize money that it stands apart in the public's mind from all others – eg the Mercantile Credit Classic, the BCE Belgian Classic, the Lada Classic, the Chipping Sodbury Classic. (ii) An adjective used by Barry Hearn to describe anything Steve Davis has just said. See also HILARIOUS.
Clean Cut	What a player's image has to be in order to attract the prestige commercial SPONSORS.
Clearance	The letter you've been waiting for from that clinic in Sheffield.
Cobblers	Another way of saying BALLS.
Commentator	A disembodied voice supplied by the BBC to make sure that viewers at home feel hopelessly inadequate in the face of his grasp of tactics and position play.
Commercials	A series of thirty second breaks in transmission of a TV programme used to remind the viewer that there is more to life than Benson & Hedges, Coral, Embassy, Goya and Lada. But not a lot.

Clearance

Commentator

Complex (i) A state-of-the-art, multi-storey snooker and leisure centre.
(ii) One of Barry Hearn's after-shave contracts.
(iii) What you develop when you're worried about the length of your CUE EXTENSION.

Concentration The ability to ignore every distraction, from the rattle of sweet papers in the back row to the stunning pair of legs in the front, and to keep one's mind firmly fixed on the immediate objective: the collection of a cheque large enough to buy the pair of legs a fur coat.

Concentration

Cue Extension

Conservative The Party most likely to win the vote of the most successful practitioners of what started as, and essentially still remains, a working man's sport. Steve Davis occupied the same stage as Bob Monkhouse and Jimmy Tarbuck at a 1983 Conservative Youth Rally at Wembley, upon Mrs Thatcher's invitation.

Contract The document a player signs to produce a bungalow for his Mum and Dad and a country estate for his MANAGER.

Crucible A thing you melt metal in.

Cue A vital piece of equipment for all players of the ball. Jimmy White often leaves his out in hotels, but Steve Davis won't let anyone touch his.

Cue Extension Device to increase the length of your cue and thus improve your performance.

D

Davis, Steve "Interesting" . . . "Hilarious" . . . Even Barry HEARN's extensive and erudite vocabulary is stretched to its very limits when trying to find words to describe the power, personality and sheer charisma of the man who is Mr Snooker to so many millions of spellbound fans.

Defeat It happens to the best of us, David. Obviously I feel a bit GUTTED, but there's nothing you can do when the boy was playing like he was today.

Deodorant	An important piece of equipment when you're reaching across to try a LONG SHOT.
Dickie, Bow	A thing around your neck.
Dickie, Davies	The last thing you'd want around your neck.
Discipline	(i) Going to bed early, wearing a collar and tie, not over-indulging in the SPONSOR'S PRODUCT, not sneaking to the NEWS OF THE WORLD. (ii) What the World Professional Snooker and Billiards Association does to you if you don't. See also DISREPUTE, BRINGING THE GAME INTO.
Discretion	Being able to tell the difference between *Cue World* and the NEWS OF THE WORLD.
Disrepute, Bringing The Game Into	Charge levied by the World Professional Snooker and Billiards Players' Association whenever they need an injection of five grand or so.
Doctor's Letter	(i) What an Irish player needs in his pocket if he is going to appear regularly at major tournaments without a tie. (ii) What an English player needs in his pocket if he is going to appear regularly at major tournaments with a mouthful of beta blockers.
Dodgy Bob	An itinerant taxi driver and impresario who took Jimmy White and Tony Meo on the money-match CIRCUIT, where Jimmy learned to count better than he could read or write.
Dope	(i) Substance applied to snooker cues. (ii) Substance applied to players' minds.

Dope

Doubles

Doubles

(i) Useful measure of play at the Jameson's International.

(ii) What you see after over-indulging in the SPONSOR'S PRODUCT.

E

Embassy

(i) The BIG ONE, the one they all want to win (despite what they tell David when they go out in the first round).

(ii) What the SAS stormed in 1981, rudely interrupting a crucial televised frame between Tony Meo and Hurricane Higgins.

Endorsement

(i) A player giving his name to a product and gaining £25,000.
(ii) A player giving his name to a magistrate and losing £250.

Exhibition

A match where a player earns twice what he'd expect to get at a tournament, and it doesn't even matter if he wins.

Exhibition

Expensive	(i) An adjective used by WHISPERING TED LOWE to describe a shot which allows a player's opponent to clear the table, win the frame and carry off the World Championship. See also BLUE. (ii) An adjective used by Barry HEARN in response to the question "How expensive would it be for Steve Davis to come and open my snooker hall?"
Expert	Anyone watching instead of playing.

Foul Stroke

Brown, Sink The

Fragrance

F

Far East	(i) A place where the exhibitions pay well, and the people eat with scaled-down snooker cues. (ii) Well beyond Romford.
Final Session	SINKING THE PINK just one more time before lights out.
Fluke	The inexplicably coincidental meeting of an Irishman's forehead with the bridge of an official's nose.
Foul Stroke	A form of perverted behaviour peculiar to chicken farmers.
Four Away	The name of a group comprising Alex Higgins, Jimmy White, Tony Knowles and Kirk Stevens who recorded one single, 'The Wanderer'. Unaccountably failing to seize the public's imagination, FOUR AWAY never even made it into the Top 50.
Fragrance	What Sharon squirts all over you as you enter the Goya Matchroom Tournament. See also DEODORANT.
Frame	(i) Fifteen minutes at the table with Steve Davis. (ii) Seven and a half minutes at the table with Jimmy White.
Framed	The innocent victim of a totally unfounded and utterly scurrilous paternity suit or drugs allegation. See also REPTILE.
Framework	(i) Apparatus for keeping certain players confined for life. (ii) Team run by Howard Kruger, comprising

anyone who couldn't make it into Barry Hearn's Matchroom organisation.

Frills What goes with the spills, eh Steve?

G

Games Boring Olympic event every four years, not worth watching until they make snooker a recognised sport.

Genesis When Genesis lead singer Phil Collins asked Steve Davis for his AUTOGRAPH in the foyer of a Glasgow hotel, he asked to borrow a pen, signed his name and sent the megastar recording artiste on his way without recognising him. When asked how he felt about it afterwards, the GINGER GIANT is said to have replied: "GUTTED."

Gentleman See also GINGER GIANT.

Ginger Giant A man from ROMFORD with an insatiable appetite for BUNGALOWS, jigsaw puzzles, origami and helping the elderly. See also GRANNY.

Glamour Finishing a match in Leeds at 2am, catching an hour's kip, driving six hours down the motorway, opening a supermarket in Chipping Sodbury, and driving back to Leeds in time to catch the FINAL SESSION.

Granny Name you call somebody who spends her life savings on a front row seat to watch Steve Davis in cabaret.

Framed

Green

Green	Anyone who plays the game for fun or for free.
Grinder	An affectionate term for Cliff Thorburn.
Groupie	See also BALL MARKER. A fan, usually female, who takes a keen interest in the finer points of the game.

Groupie

Hairdresser

Gutted
(i) Broken by defeat.
(ii) Bearing a marked resemblance to Bill Werbeniuk.

Gwonmyson
An expression of encouragement given to snooker players at crucial moments during a big match.

H

Hairdresser
An affectionate term for a player without a CUE EXTENSION.

Half-Butt	(i) That portion of the cigarette that sits in the ashtray between trips to the table. (ii) All that's left in Bill Werbeniuk's trousers when he has to really reach for the white.
Half-Pint	Unit of liquid measure unheard of north of Watford.
Half-Size	See HAIRDRESSER.
Handshake	According to MR BIG Barry Hearn, when he first met Steve Davis, shaking hands with the awkward ROMFORD lad was like strangling a cabbage. This must have been the time the Darryl Zanuck of snooker decided always to use CONTRACTS.
Hearn	(i) According to some, the man who did for snooker what Mark McCormack did for golf. (ii) According to some, the man who did for snooker.
Hexagon	Snooker table built to EEC specifications.
Hilarious	Word used regularly by Barry Hearn to describe Steve Davis's devastating repartee.
Hot Pot	(i) A dish enjoyed by Lancastrian players. (ii) An affectionate term for Tony Knowles – 'the hottest pot in snooker'.
Hurricane	To play PHENOMENALLY so that you manage a break of 30 or so in as many seconds, before storming back to your seat and brooding heavily as you light up yet another Benson & Hedges.
Hustler	A lady who makes a living by picking up snooker players in the hotel lobby.

Hexagon

I

Image

It's all a question of the right shoes, suit and haircut if you want to crack the big Swiss watch sponsorship deal or stay on WHISPERING TED LOWE's Christmas card list. If you don't, it's easy. Just call yourself Alex "KERRYGOLD" Higgins.

Interesting

According to those who know him, there are three Steve Davises. Steve "Interesting" Davis is the one the viewers see being interviewed by David VINE, or cracking jokes (see also HILARIOUS) at sponsor's promotional dinners. At home he is much more shy and retiring.

International	Bigger than King Size.
Interview	An opportunity to tell David VINE three or four times how you feel after losing the World Championship on the last ball. See also BLUE.
Italian Stallion	Fortunately, the only thing Tony Meo and Sylvester Stallone have in common is their nickname. When terrorists are at large (see EMBASSY) Tony plays snooker. Sly hides under the table.

J

Jimmy	What players go for in the interval.
Jump	Result of a successful LONG SHOT.

Jimmy

K

Kerrygold
(i) The best butter in Ireland.
(ii) An affectionate nickname for Hurricane Higgins.

Kick
(i) To give up a habit that is both expensive, and harmful to one's nasal cavities – or at least, to tell the NEWS OF THE WORLD that you have.
(ii) What you do to over-inquisitive journalists from the newspaper that didn't buy the exclusive.

Kiss
Term used to describe that moment when the player's balls get so close that they actually touch. In snooker, unlike soccer, this occurs relatively infrequently and is governed by rules strictly enforced by the referee.

Hurricane

Knickers	Exhibit A in one of a whole series of newspaper exposures of Tony Knowles's life in–between EXHIBITIONS.
Kray	Ronald and Reginald Kray owned The Regal Billiards Hall in the East End of London throughout the 1950s. Keen aficionados of the game, Ronnie and Reggie played host to many up-and-coming players, and were responsible in no small way for the IMAGE of snooker before they took the LONG REST.

L

Lager	Amber liquid poured over opponent's head upon unsuccessful conclusion of final frame. See also LOSING.
Leg Over	Technique employed to relieve an uncomfortable ball position.
Leisure Investments	An important part of any player's portfolio – a balanced financial interest in everything from FRAGRANCES to one-armed bandits.
Long Butt	(i) Dunhill International. (ii) The inevitable result of a big argument with an emotional player.
Long Rest	(i) The inevitable result of a LONG BUTT. (ii) The space between a LONG BUTT and the next time an emotional player is allowed to play another tournament. (iii) Several years at Her Majesty's pleasure. See also KRAY.

Leg Over

Long Shot

(i) You spot this incredibly attractive BALL MARKER in the audience, make your way over to her and say: 'My name is Steve Davis. What are you doing for dinner tonight?'

(ii) You spot your manager on the way to the restaurant and say: 'Looks like I might get lucky later on Barry. Do you think I can borrow a twenty?'

Long Tackle

See also CUE EXTENSION and BOLTON HEART THROB.

Loose Reds

(i) Voluptuous Russian BALL MARKERS. See also FAR EAST.

(ii) What, allegedly, you find in the bottom of some players' washbags, along with the beta blockers, bottles of Goya and pairs of ladies' KNICKERS.

Loose Reds

Losing	An unfortunate climax to a fortnight in which your mother died, your favourite CUE got stolen and some rotten little BALL MARKER revealed the secrets of your CUE EXTENSION to the NEWS OF THE WORLD.
Lucania	Exotic name for Barry Hearn's chain of snooker halls which has its headquarters in ROMFORD.

Long Tackle

Losing

Machine-Gun Shot

M

Machine-Gun Shot

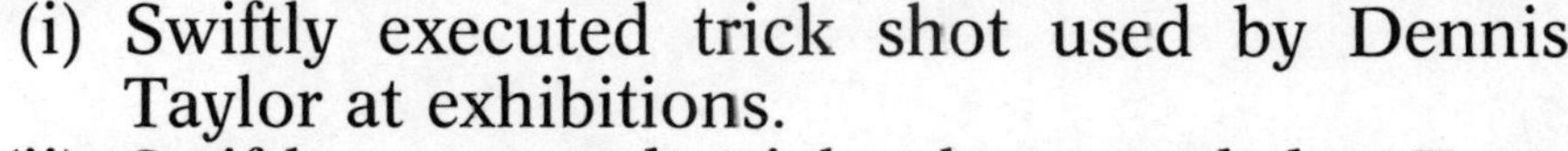

(i) Swiftly executed trick shot used by Dennis Taylor at exhibitions.
(ii) Swiftly executed trick shot used by Tony Knowles between exhibitions.

Far East

Manager

Mafia — Men in black shirts and white ties who run the Steve Davis souvenir stall.

Manager —
(i) A man who taps you on the shoulder between frames at the Romford Social Club and promises you fame, fortune, fragrances and as much lager as you can drink.
(ii) A man who taps you on the shoulder between frames at the Romford Social club and promises that if you pour one more pint over your opponent's head, two of the balls on the table will be yours.

Matchroom Group of men, under exclusive contract to Barry Hearn, whose job it is to open Far Eastern snooker halls and to autograph packaging for ranges of international fragrances.

Medallion Gold jewellery, often a Krugerrand or genuine hall-marked ingot from the Franklin Mint, worn with one's shirt open to the navel to emphasise one's luxuriant endowment of chest hair. No need to see GINGER GIANT.

Media Methods of communicating one's most profound thoughts and ideas, with the help of a ghost writer.

Merchandise What you trip over when attempting to effect a hurried exit from the Crucible Theatre. See also MAFIA.

Millionaire Adjective to describe any friend of Barry Hearn's.

Miscue
(i) To fluff a shot.
(ii) To order a camera shot of Steve Davis potting the black when the SPONSOR's instructions clearly require a close-up of Alex Higgins chain smoking.

Mr Big An affectionate term for Barry Hearn, the mastermind behind MATCHROOM.

N

Nap Short rest between visits to the table whilst a player is waiting for someone to bring him another pack of Rothmans. See also ZZZZ.

Medallion

Miscue

News of the World Another name for the popular Sunday newspaper, 'News of the Screws', so called because of its detailed snooker coverage.

Noddies (As in Doing the Noddies) Substitute for conversation used whenever a man approaches you with a microphone and asks you if you're looking forward to opening the Chung Li Snooker Centre in Kowloon, if you're jealous of Steve Davis's Porsche, or if you'd like another pack of Rothmans.

O

Olympics
(i) What happens in Seoul in 1988.
(ii) What happens in Tenerife every time Tony Knowles goes on holiday.

Organ An instrument made by Yamaha, sponsors of the Yamaha Organs International Masters. See also NEWS OF THE WORLD.

Oswaldtwistle The original home of the PEOPLE'S CHAMPION.

P

Pack
(i) The collective name for a group of LOOSE REDS.
(ii) The most convenient receptacle for any Rothmans that don't end up in the ASHTRAY.
(iii) The only thing left to do after the referee has been on the business end of another LONG BUTT.

Personality

Packet	(i) A small pack. (ii) A large cheque.
Percentage	Term applied to the sum of money removed from your winnings by your manager, that is somehow always substantial enough to ensure that he drives the Porsche and you hitch the lift.
Percentage Play	The way to play if you want to increase your percentage.
Personality	Type of player who urinates in the sponsor's plant pots, brings the game into disrepute, and guarantees the highest television viewing figures of any sport in the world.
Phenomenal	An adjective Alex Higgins often uses to describe himself.
Pillow	What HAIRDRESSERS use instead of BAULK CUSHIONS.
Pink	Mild shade of red which suffuses the cheek after excessive enjoyment of the SPONSOR'S product.
Plant	See VINE.
Player	A brand of cigarette.
Pocket	(i) Where to put your winnings before the Inland Revenue sees them. (ii) Where to put your hand when confronted by a difficult touching ball.
Pocket Billiards	(i) Curious American variation on the game of snooker, made popular by Paul Newman and Edward G. Robinson. (ii) Game played by people with very small balls.

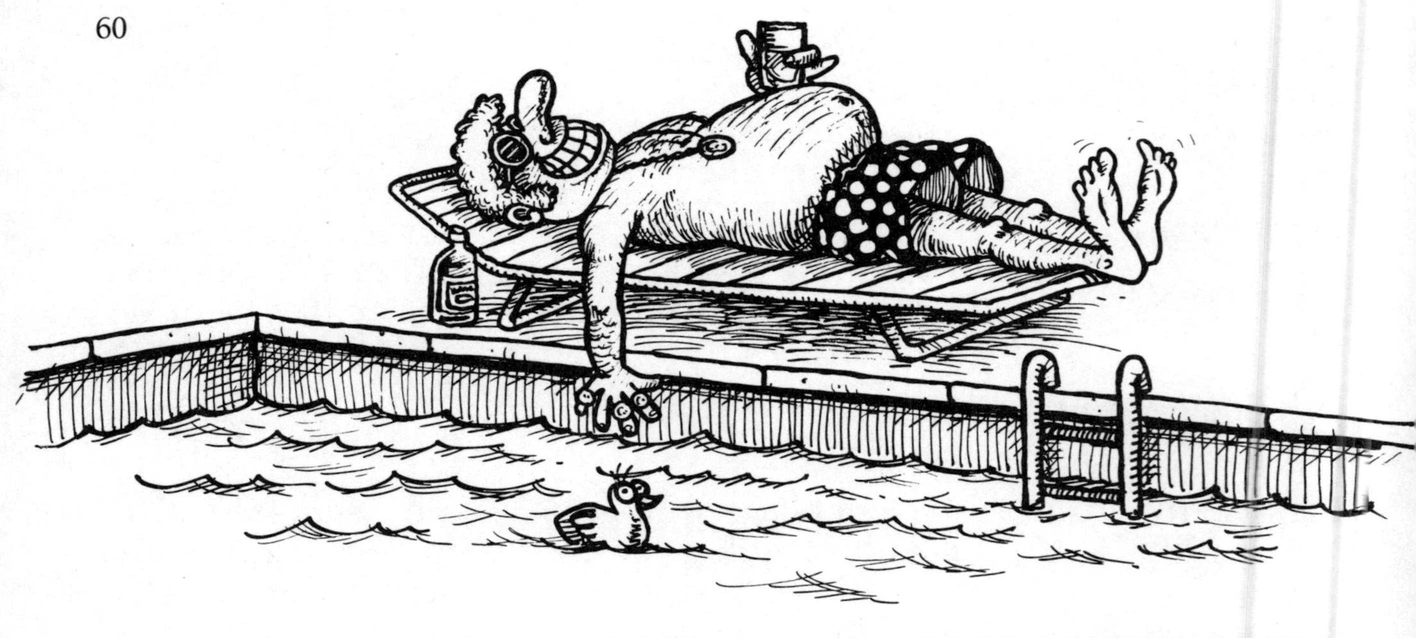

Pool (See also Pocket Billiards)	(i) The next thing a player buys after the Porsche and the BUNGALOW when he wins the BIG ONE. (ii) The next thing he jumps into when Dennis Taylor knocks him out of the BIG ONE.
Pot	(i) That portion of the player's anatomy, which comes to rest on the edge of the table when he takes up cue position. (ii) That portion of the player's winnings which reaches him after deductions are made by his manager, his accountant, landlord and his ex-wife. (See also GUTTED).
Psychiatrist	A man with a beard, steel-rimmed spectacles and a heavy Viennese accent who can use nine-syllable words to unravel the arcane symbolism of CUE and BALL, but remains completely baffled by an emotional player's behaviour when confronted with a sponsor's plant pot.

Pusher	(i) One who favours the PUSH SHOT. (ii) One who gives their child snooker lessons at the age of three. (iii) One who supplies LOOSE REDS.
Push Shot	A milder alternative to the LONG BUTT, and generally applied to the area of your opponent's lapels.
Putting One's Opponent in Again	Inviting one's opponent to return to the table so that one can have enough time to finish one's lager, and, with any luck, his as well.

Plant

Pot

Q

Queue

(i) A line of people waiting anxiously for a JIMMY after sampling the SPONSOR'S PRODUCT a little over-enthusiastically.
(ii) A line of people waiting anxiously to leave the Crucible by the only exit not barricaded by Steve Davis souvenir stalls. See also MAFIA.
(iii) The best way to spell 'cue' if you've got a 'Q', two 'U's, two 'E's and a chance at a triple word score.

R

Ranking

(i) Measure of a player's success at the table during a given year.
(ii) Fiendish oriental version of POCKET BILLIARDS. See also FAR EAST.

Red

(i) The colour a player's manager goes if he mentions the word 'audit' twice. See also PINK.
(ii) As in Jimmy White's answer to the question: "Jimmy, are you well-read?" – "Yeah, I mean yesterday I ran up the stairs fast and I was well red."

Reptile

(i) A fashionable adornment for a designer sports shirt which says: "I've arrived."
(ii) The name you call the *News Of The World* reporter who says: "But you won't be around for long."

Re-Spotting

Rest	Something to catch up on during *A Frame With Davis.*
Rest Home	Where you'll end up if you ignore the previous piece of advice.
Re-Spotting	Judicious application of 5 and 9 by the make-up girl before you go back in front of the cameras.
Romford	Celebrated Mecca for lovers of John Bull bitter, Goya MATCHROOM, wit, repartee, neat THREADS and Steve DAVIS.
Roots	(i) Nature's way of telling you it's time to stop using Terry Griffiths' hairdresser. (ii) Nature's way of telling you you'll never escape from ROMFORD. (iii) Nature's way of telling you there's more than one way of SINKING THE PINK.
Royalty	(i) The House of Windsor. (ii) The House of Romford. (iii) The only thing worth leaving home for.
Ruff	(i) Snappy fashion accessory on front of dress shirt. See also FRILLS. (ii) How a player feels after a big FINAL SESSION.

S

Safety Shot Sinking the pink with your LONG TACKLE protected by rubber.

Screw
(i) What you try to apply to the cue ball because it's what Ted Lowe says will help position it for the next shot, but which instead sends it skidding crazily out of control across the table, disturbing the reds, potting the black, and losing you eight points.
(ii) An expression of displeasure on being knocked out of the first round.
(iii) All you can do for the next two weeks, especially in Sheffield.

Session Getting stuck into the sponsor's product before, during and after the match.

Sex As any PSYCHIATRIST will tell you, it's the most important ingredient of the snooker cocktail.
As any REPTILE will tell you, it's the *only* ingredient of the snooker cocktail.
See also BOLTON HEART THROB.

Shoot
(i) What you do to the ball between rests.
(ii) What you do to your cuffs between balls.
(iii) What you do to yourself when you get more rests than balls.

Sign
(i) A large hoarding decorated with the words Benson & Hedges, Jameson's International, Lada Classic, or similar.

Jump Shot

	(ii) An unequivocal instruction from your MANAGER, delivered as your pen hovers uncertainly over the CONTRACT that gives him 90% of the proceeds from a deal with Benson & Hedges, Jameson's, Lada or similar, and you 10%.
Signing	Something a player spends his time doing between tournaments, on anything from CUES to AUTOBIOGRAPHIES, or PACKETS of after-shave if he has a CONTRACT with Goya which gives him ROYALTIES from the sales of their international FRAGRANCES.
Sink	An item of hotel furniture that comes into its own when you've sampled too much of the SPONSOR'S PRODUCT.
Sinking The Pink	Method of ensuring that there are future generations of snooker players.
Slate	Ideal surface on which players may record the level of their consumption of the sponsor's product during a single SESSION.
Slate Bed	The centre of a snooker player's dilemma. You can't lie on it, but it's the only surface that allows total control of the ball.
Small Beer	(i) Anyone who isn't Steve Davis. (ii) See also HALF-PINT.
Snooker	A gruelling test of endurance in which millions of people must stay awake all night for two weeks, until a man with red hair and half a dinner suit smiles and picks up a large cheque.

Ruff

Sponsor's Product

Snookered	Being put in a position by one's opponent that is so irredeemable that the only way out is a LONG BUTT or PUSH SHOT.
Spider	Six legged arachnid that makes its home in the pockets of very old snooker players.
Sponsor	Manufacturer of cigarettes or alcohol, or any other substance which cannot legally be advertised on television.
Sponsor's Product	Perishable goods provided by tobacco manufacturers and distillers for the enjoyment of players in–between visits to the table.
Sporting Cabaret	A lucrative promotional extravaganza involving the gathering together of SMALL BEER and GRANNIES in the velour-upholstered confines of a suitable leisure COMPLEX, with the express purpose of paying money in order to listen to Steve Davis being INTERESTING and HILARIOUS.
Spot	A small eruption at the corner of one's mouth that prompts a couple of angry phone calls to Sheffield.
Square One	Where a player goes back to if a major daily newspaper says he wears women's KNICKERS and the SPONSOR withdraws his PRODUCT.
Statistics	(i) Vital measurement of a player's success, employed to persuade SPONSORS and leisure investors to put his name on their PRODUCTS and their name on his cheques. (ii) Vital measurement of CUE EXTENSION if a player is to achieve satisfactory RANKING.

Stevemobile	Wheels, a means of getting down to one's favourite record store in ROMFORD. Originally a CADILLAC, since traded in for a Porsche.
Sticks	(i) Vernacular synonym for 'cues'. (ii) What they use in Hong Kong instead of knives and forks. (iii) Affectionate description of the countryside surrounding Romford.
Strings	Often invisible appendages to players' CONTRACTS designed to tie them up in knots. See also ANGLES, PERCENTAGE and MANAGER.
Stuck	The result of a difficult ball position.
Stud	(i) An item of jewellery for fastening one's cuffs. (ii) That's enough Tony Knowles jokes. Ed.
Stunner	The BALL MARKER in the front row with the Page 3 smile.
Succeed	What a toothless budgie does.
Super square	Steve Davis's haircut.
Swerve	A loose-limbed movement employed by a player attempting to return to his hotel after a big SESSION.

T

Table	A low, squarish item of furniture on which to place the ASHTRAY, the LAGER, and the EMBASSY.
Tantrum	Alex Higgins's favourite response to being told: to wear a tie; its bedtime; we're closed; you've lost.

Spot

Touching Ball

Thin Cut	A dress suit that has failed to expand at the same rate as its wearer. See also WERBENIUK.
Threads	Snappy gear to play snooker and attract BALL MARKERS.
Thumb Print	Jimmy White's autograph.
Touching Ball	Alleviating an uncomfortable ball position with a bit of wrist.
Triangle	A piece of equipment that helps you position your balls.
Tribunal	A group of snooker's elder statesmen which convenes whenever a player "brings the game into DISREPUTE" by telling the newspapers what the game is really like. See also KNICKERS, NEWS OF THE WORLD, and CUE EXTENSION.
Triffic	An adjective Steve Davis uses instead of PHENOMENAL.

U

Untamed	Jimmy White's, Kirk Stevens's, Alex Higgins's and Tony Knowles' CUE EXTENSION.
Upmarket	The only word to describe a game where much the most INTERESTING players have short hair, immaculate dinner suits, impeccable manners, incalculable bank balances, fabulous motors and it's just the others who go round giving referees the LONG BUTT and wearing women's KNICKERS.

V

Verbals — Not to be confused with cuebals or objectbals, verbals are generally more profitably employed off the table, where they result in large CHEQUES and LEISURE INVESTMENTS, rather than on the table, where they result in TANTRUMS, LONG BUTTS and TRIBUNALS.

Vine — A type of creeper. See also PLANT and REPTILE.

Volume
 (i) An AUTOBIOGRAPHY.
 (ii) What a manufacturer sells of anything with Steve Davis's name on it.

W

Waistcoat — An item of attire insisted upon by WHISPERING TED LOWE right from the first transmission of POT BLACK, to which he ascribes the achievement of snooker's UPMARKET IMAGE.

Wally — Name of Joe Johnson's manager before he won the BIG ONE.

Walter — Name of Joe Johnson's manger after he won the BIG ONE.

Wally — Name of Joe Johnson's manager after he lost Joe Johnson.

Werbeniuk — A Canadian exercise, whereby the player lifts his elbow eight or nine times before commencing a frame, tilting a pint of lager down his throat at the top of each lift.

Verbals

Whirlwind	An affectionate term for Jimmy White. See also HURRICANE.
Whispering Ted Lowe	The man who put the CLASS into CLASSIC, and the boot in Alex Higgins, whom he banned from POT BLACK for a five year stretch. See also LONG REST. Ted is unquestionably the voice of snooker, whose smooth, modulated commentaries and unswerving loyalty to the game make him the last word in SNOOKER. Oh, except for these other ones that I had to use to get to the end of the alphabet.
Willie	A shiny headed chap who SINKS THE PINK.
Women	People who are unable to play snooker because of certain natural protuberances that either block their view or smother the LOOSE REDS.
Wrist	The thing a player uses to apply a bit of twist or spin to the end of the LONG TACKLE when he is faced with a BLUE BALL or when a BALL MARKER is not available.

Y

Yellow	How to tell lager from Bacardi and Coke.
Youth, Misspent	What people used to say playing snooker well was a sign of – until the boys started earning more in a day than most of those people earned in an entire year.

Z

ZZZZZZ	Noise emanating from a television viewer while watching *A Frame With Davis.*

ZZZZZ